BRAZIL

LETTERS FROM AROUND THE WORLD

Patrick Cunningham

Photographs by Sue Cunningham

CHERRYTREE BOOKS

Distributed in the United States by
Cherrytree Books
1980 Lookout Drive
North Mankato, MN 56001

U.S. publication copyright © Cherrytree Books 2005
International copyright reserved in all countries. No part of
this book may be reproduced in any form without written
permission from the publisher.

Library of Congress Cataloging-in-Publication Data
Cunningham, Patrick
   Brazil / by Patrick Cunningham
     p.cm. – (Letters from around the world)
   Includes index.
   ISBN 1-84234-253-3 (alk. paper)
     1. Brazil--Social life and customs--Juvenile literature.
     2. Brazil--Description and travel--Juvenile literature.
   I. Title. II. Series.

F2510.C865 2004
981--dc22

2004041343

First Edition
9 8 7 6 5 4 3 2 1

First published in 2004 by
Evans Brothers Ltd
2A Portman Mansions
Chiltern Street
London W1U 6NR

© Copyright Evans Brothers Limited 2004

Conceived and produced by

Nutshell
MEDIA

www.nutshellmedialtd.co.uk

Editor: Polly Goodman
Design: Mayer Media Ltd
Cartography: Encompass Graphics Ltd
Artwork: Mayer Media Ltd
Consultants: Jeff Stanfield and Anne Spiring

All photographs were taken by Julio Etchart,
   except: pp 8 & 29 (left): Jimmy Holmes.

Printed in Hong Kong.

Acknowledgments
The photographer would like to thank the Soriano family,
the Fernandes family and the staff and students of Rio de
Janeiro School for their help with this book.

Cover: Julio (center) with his friends Daniel and Salvatore
   on Copacabana Beach.
Title page: Julio (left) with his friends João and Lucas
   swinging in a hammock.
This page: A flooded part of the Amazon rain forest.
Contents page: Julio practices a handstand.
Glossary page: Parrots in Rio's Botanical Gardens.
Further Information page: Iguaçu Falls.
Index: A game of soccer on Ipanema Beach.

Contents

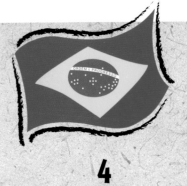

My Country	4
Landscape and Weather	8
At Home	10
Food and Mealtimes	14
School Day	18
Off to Work	22
Free Time	24
Religion and Festivals	26
Fact File	28
Glossary	30
Further Information	31
Index	32

My Country

Saturday, May 3

Avenida Borges 6412
Apartment 347
Rio de Janeiro, RJ
CEP 23129-000
Brazil

Dear Jo,

Bom Dia! (You say "Bom jee-ah." This means "good day" or "hello" in Portuguese, Brazil's main language.)

My name's Julio Soriano and I'm 8 years old. I live in Rio de Janeiro, a big city in Brazil. We call it Rio for short. I have one little sister, Sofia, who is 4.

I can help you with your class projects on Brazil.

Write back soon!

From

Julio

This is me with Sofia, Mom, and Dad, outside our flat.

Brazil is so big that both the Equator and the Tropic of Capricorn run across it.

Brazil's place in the world.

COLOMBIA

VENEZUELA

GUYANA

SURINAME

French Guiana

PERU

Equator

△ Pico da Neblina
9,886 ft (3,014 m)

Manaus

Amazon

Belém

Amazon

Fortaleza

AMAZON RAIN FOREST

B R A Z I L

Recife

PERU

São Francisco

Salvador

BOLIVIA

BRASÍLIA

Belo Horizonte

N

PARAGUAY

Tropic of Capricorn

São Paulo

Rio de Janeiro

Iguaçu Falls

Curitiba

ATLANTIC OCEAN

ARGENTINA

URUGUAY

Porto Alegre

| 0 | 200 | 400 | 600 | 800 kilometers |
| 0 | 200 | | 400 miles | |

Brazil is the biggest country in South America and the fifth-largest country in the world. It has borders with 10 other countries.

Rio de Janeiro means "River of January" because in January 1502, Portuguese explorers thought they had discovered the mouth of a river. But Rio is on a big bay, not a rivermouth.

High-rise office and apartment buildings are squeezed between Rio's hills.

Rio used to be the capital of Brazil. In the late 1950s, a new capital city called Brasília was built in the middle of the country. Rio is still an important business center and a busy port.

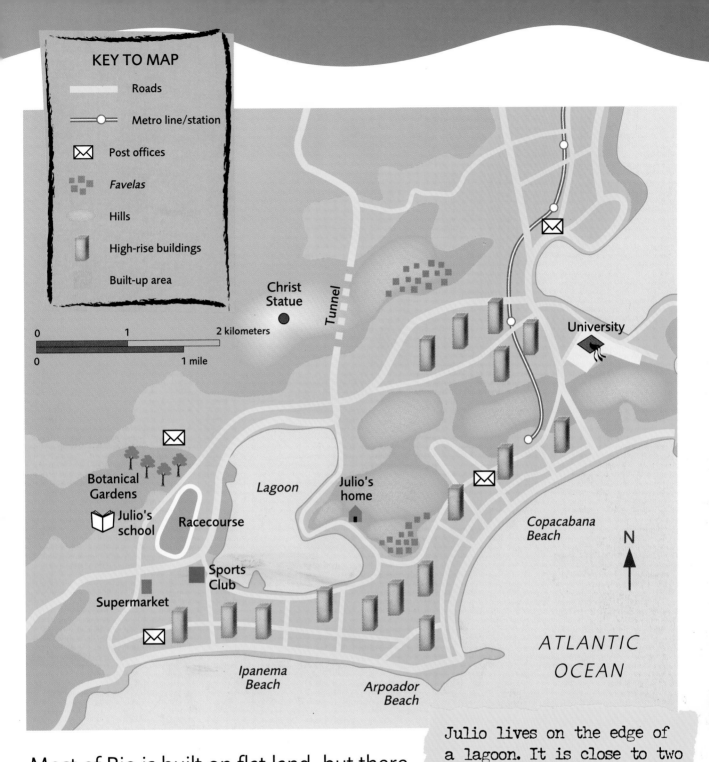

KEY TO MAP

- Roads
- Metro line/station
- ✉ Post offices
- *Favelas*
- Hills
- High-rise buildings
- Built-up area

Christ Statue

Tunnel

University

2 kilometers
1 mile

Botanical Gardens

Julio's school

Racecourse

Lagoon

Julio's home

Copacabana Beach

N

Sports Club

Supermarket

Ipanema Beach

Arpoador Beach

ATLANTIC OCEAN

Julio lives on the edge of a lagoon. It is close to two of Rio's biggest beaches, Copacabana and Ipanema.

Most of Rio is built on flat land, but there are several steep hills. Poor people build their homes on the hillsides, in areas called *favelas* (you say "fa-vell-ah"). The streets of Rio are often jammed with traffic. It can be quicker to use the train to get around.

Landscape and Weather

Rio is one of many natural harbors on Brazil's long coastline. Outside the city there are coffee and sugarcane plantations. In the north of Brazil is the vast Amazon rain forest.

Rio is in the tropics, so it is hot all year round. In tropical storms it can rain very hard. Houses in Rio's *favelas* sometimes get washed away in the floods.

Large areas of the Amazon rain forest are flooded for part of each year.

Rio is lined with long sandy beaches and rocky shores.

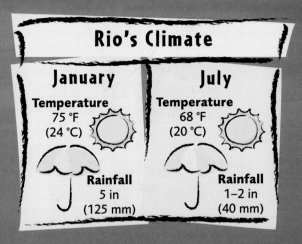

Rio's Climate

January	July
Temperature 75 °F (24 °C)	**Temperature** 68 °F (20 °C)
Rainfall 5 in (125 mm)	**Rainfall** 1–2 in (40 mm)

ESCOLINHA Fla
ESCOLA OFICIAL
DO FLAMENGO

At Home

Like most people in Rio, Julio's family lives in an apartment. It is on the fourth floor of a tall building, beside a lagoon. There are three other apartments on the same floor. The building has 11 floors altogether.

This is the view from Julio's apartment. You can see across the lagoon and the high-rise buildings to the sea the other side.

When Julio's grandmother comes to visit, the family often sits out on the balcony.

Julio's apartment has two bedrooms, a living room, a kitchen, and two bathrooms. There is also a small study. Outside there is a balcony, with a high fence to stop anyone from falling over the railing.

The living room has a television, VCR, stereo, and Julio's computer game.

Julio and Sofia share a bedroom. They can see right across the lagoon from their bedroom window. If he goes to bed after Sofia is asleep, Julio has to be really quiet.

Julio's dad has a computer in the study. Sometimes he lets Julio play games on it.

Monday, July 7

Avenida Borges 6412
Apartment 347
Rio de Janeiro, RJ
CEP 23129-000
Brazil

Oba! (You say "or-ba." This means "hi" in Portuguese.)

It was great to get your letter yesterday. Have I told you about the play area we've got at home? It's on the ground floor of our apartment building. There are swings and a slide, which Sofia likes, but I prefer the foosball table. The floor's really smooth for practicing skateboard tricks, too.

Write again soon!

From
Julio

Here I am playing table soccer with Dad.

Food and Mealtimes

Julio's family usually has lunch together. Maria the maid helps prepare the food.

For breakfast, Julio has cereal and a milkshake. Lunch can be chicken and salad or fresh vegetables. Black beans and rice is a favorite Brazilian dish.

In the evening, Julio's family sometimes has fish with *mandioca frita* — fried cassava chips. There is always lots of fresh fruit.

Julio's mom does most of the shopping in the local supermarket. Sometimes she buys fruit and vegetables from market stands, which are set up every Saturday near the apartment.

In the supermarket, people use the *real* (you say "ray-al") to buy food. The *real* is the currency in Brazil.

Julio buys a coconut with its top cut off so he can drink the juice through a straw.

15

Thursday, August 21

Avenida Borges 6412
Apartment 347
Rio de Janeiro, RJ
CEP 23129-000.
Brazil

Hi Jo,

Thanks for the recipe you sent me. Here's one for you. It's for Brazilian candies, called brigadeiros (you say "brig-a-dare-us"):

You will need: 1 can sweetened condensed milk,
8 teaspoons cocoa powder, 1 tablespoon butter,
grated chocolate

1. Put the condensed milk in a saucepan with the butter.
2. Stir over a medium heat until the butter has melted.

3. Add the cocoa powder
   and stir until it goes gooey.
4. Remove from the heat
   and let the mixture cool.

← This is my grandma
   helping me stir the
   chocolate mixture.

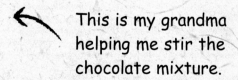

Everyone likes rolling the chocolate balls. It's very tempting to lick your fingers!

5. Take a teaspoonful of the mixture and roll it into a ball.

6. Roll the ball in the grated chocolate and put it on a plate.

7. Do the same until all the mixture has been used.

Write and tell me what you think of them.

From

Julio

Lots of brigadeiros, ready to be eaten — yummy!

School Day

In Brazil, some children go to school in the morning and some go in the afternoon. Julio goes to school from 1 p.m. until 5:15 p.m. His dad usually drives him there after lunch, on his way back to work.

Children who live nearby walk to school. Others travel by car or by minibus.

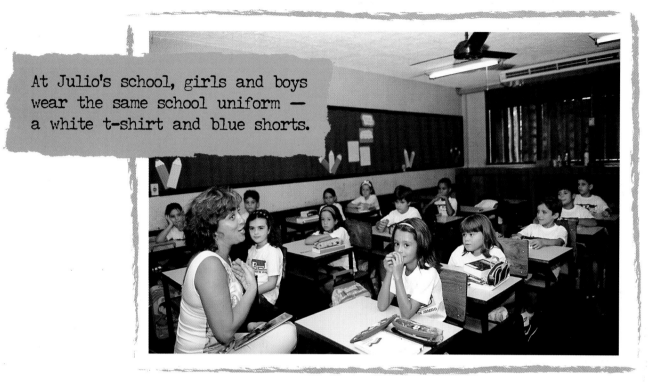

At Julio's school, girls and boys wear the same school uniform — a white t-shirt and blue shorts.

Julio's class learns English, math, science, history, geography, music, and art. They also learn Portuguese, which is Brazil's main language.

Julio and his friends Lucas and Pedro draw pictures in an art class.

Julio's class does projects in the school library.

The long school vacation is in the Brazilian summer, from mid-December to the end of January. There is also a winter break of three or four weeks in July.

Julio's class often studies math outside. Here Julio is learning about tens and hundreds.

Friday, December 5

Avenida Borges 6412
Apartment 347
Rio de Janeiro, RJ
CEP 23129-000
Brazil

Bom Dia Jo!

I'm glad you liked the *brigadeiros*. At school this week we did a project about teeth. They're called *dentes* (you say "den-chis") in Portuguese. We made a poster with a diagram of a tooth and the names of all the different teeth. We included photos of food that is good for your teeth, like fruit and vegetables. I'm going to try not to eat too much candy because it rots your teeth. Then you have to go to the dentist and have a filling.

Write soon!

From
Julio

This is the poster we made for our teeth project.

Off to Work

Julio's dad is a lecturer at Rio's university. He teaches his students about tourism. When they finish college, some of the students will work in hotels and travel agencies. Some will become tour guides, helping vacationers who visit Rio.

Julio's dad teaches his students in a classroom at the university.

This trader is selling towels to tourists on Copacabana Beach.

Lots of people work in offices in Rio. The city is an important business center. Other people in Rio work in stores or factories.

Outside Rio, this man is squeezing the juice out of sugarcane. It will be sold as a drink.

Outside the city, there are lots of jobs on plantations growing oranges, coffee, and sugarcane. Orange juice from Brazil is exported all around the world.

23

Free Time

Julio and his friend Lucas see who can do a handstand for the longest. Julio's record is 9 seconds.

Everyone in Rio loves the beach. Whenever he can, Julio goes there to surf, or just to play on the sand.

Sometimes Julio goes to the sports club just across the lagoon from home. He can play tennis and swim in the pool there.

Volleyball is a popular game on Rio's beaches.

Julio's family often visits the Botanical Gardens. There are lots of flowers, trees, monkeys, and colorful parrots to see.

Colorful parrots and other birds fly around high in the trees of the Botanical Gardens.

Religion and Festivals

The Christ Statue is on the highest hill in Rio. It overlooks the whole city.

Most Brazilians are Roman Catholics, but there are other religions, too. Many people whose ancestors were African still follow African religions.

Everyone takes part in the Carnival celebrations in February. The whole country has a holiday. The last day of Carnival is Shrove Tuesday.

These girls are dressed in their special Carnival costumes.

Sunday, February 14

Avenida Borges 6412
Apartment 347
Rio de Janeiro, RJ
CEP 23129-000
Brazil

Hi Jo,

It's been really exciting here because it's Carnival time! Last Friday we went to watch the big procession through the streets. Everyone dressed up. I wore the Carnival costume that Mom helped me to make. The noise of the drumming was deafening. I had to stick my fingers in my ears! Everyone on the street was dancing samba. The next day we went to a Carnival party. There were lots of musicians playing samba tunes.

Do you celebrate any special festivals?

From
Julio

These costumes were amazing!

Fact File

Size: 3,285,622 square miles (8,547,404 km^2).

Population: 170.1 million. Brazil has the world's fifth-largest population.

Flag: The green and yellow colors stand for forests and minerals. Inside the yellow diamond is a blue sphere, with a star for each of the 26 states and Brasilia's Federal District. Across the sphere is written the motto *Ordem e progresso*, which means "order and progress."

Capital City: Brasília is the capital of Brazil. It was built in the 1950s in the middle of the country. Before Brasília, Rio was the capital, and before Rio the capital was Salvador.

Other Major Cities: São Paulo is Brazil's biggest city. Rio de Janeiro is the second-biggest city. Other major cities are Belo Horizonte, Salvador, Fortaleza, Curitiba, Recife, Porto Alegre, Belém, and Manaus.

Neighboring Countries: French Guiana, Suriname, Guyana, Venezuela, Colombia, Peru, Bolivia, Paraguay, Argentina, and Uruguay.

Languages: Portuguese is the main language. There are also about 120 native Amerindian languages. Immigrant groups speak their own languages as well as Portuguese. Some of these are Japanese, Italian, and German.

Highest Mountain: Pico da Neblina 9,886 feet (3,014 m).

Currency: The *real* (R$). There are 100 centavos to one *real*.

Longest River: The Amazon is 6,577 km long. It is the second-longest river in the world. Ocean-going ships can navigate much of the Amazon in Brazil.

Biggest Waterfall: The Iguaçu Falls are one of the natural wonders of the world. They fall over the border between Brazil and Argentina.

Main Industries: Iron, steel and aluminum, motor vehicles, electronic goods, coffee, sugar, orange juice, and soy beans.

Famous Brazilians: Alberto Santos Dumont was one of the first people to make and fly an airplane, in 1906. Many people say that Pelé was the greatest soccer player ever.

Main Religions: Most Brazilians are Roman Catholic, but there are also Muslims, Jews, and Shinto followers. In the northeast, many people still follow African religions, such as Candomblé and Umbanda.

Stamps: Brazilian stamps often show Brazil's wildlife, or musical instruments that are used to play Brazilian music.

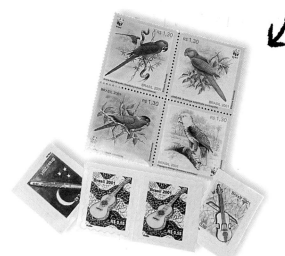

Glossary

Amerindian The name given to the people who were already living in South America before explorers arrived from Spain and Portugal.

ancestors People who lived before you, from whom you are directly descended. Your grandparents are your ancestors.

Bom Dia (you say "Bom jee-ah") The greeting used by Brazilians in the morning. It means "Good day."

Carnival The most important Brazilian festival, 40 days before Easter. Processions of decorated trucks tour the streets. People dress up in fancy dress and there is lots of music.

cassava A root vegetable, like potatoes.

Equator An imaginary line that runs around the middle of the Earth.

exported Sold abroad.

favela An area of cheap housing built by poor people.

lagoon A lake connected to the sea or a bigger area of water.

metro A subway system.

plantations Large farms where only one crop is grown.

procession A large number of people moving together.

rivermouth The part of a river where it meets the sea.

samba A Brazilian dance with an offbeat rhythm that started in Africa.

sugarcane Tall grass that contains sugar in its sap.

tourism The business of providing services to vacationers.

Tropics The regions either side of the Equator, between the Tropics of Cancer and Capricorn.

Further Information

Information books:

Campos, Maria de Fatima. *B is for Brazil*. Parsippany, NJ: Silver Press, 1999.

Fox, Mary Virginia. *Continents: South America*. Chicago: Heinemann, 2002.

Lichtenberg, Andre. *We Come from Brazil*. Chicago: Raintree/Steck-Vaughn, 2000.

Morrison, Marion. *Country Insights: Brazil*. London: Hodder & Stoughton, 1999.

Parker, Edward. *The Changing Face of Brazil*. Chicago: Raintree/Steck-Vaughn, 2002.

Phillips, C. *Fiesta!: Brazil*. London: Franklin Watts, 2001.

Serra, Mariana. *A Flavour of Brazil*. London: Hodder & Stoughton, 1999.

Fiction:

Gerson, Mary-Joan. *How Night Came from the Sea: A Story from Brazil*. Little, Brown & Co, 1994.

Lippert, Margaret H. *The Sea Serpent's Daughter: A Brazilian Legend*. Bridgewater Books, 1993.

Web sites:

CIA Factbook
www.cia.gov/cia/publications/factbook/
Basic facts and figures about Brazil and other countries.

Viva Brazil.com
www.vivabrazil.com
A virtual trip to Brazil.

Index

Numbers in **bold** refer to photographs and illustrations.

beaches **7**, **9**, **23**, **24**, **25**

cities
 Brasília **5**, 6, **28**
 Rio de Janeiro 4, **5**, **6**, **7**, 8, **9**, 10, 22, 23, **24**, **25**, **26**, 28
clothes **19**, **26**, **27**
currency 15, **29**

Equator **5**

family **4**, 10, **11**, **12**, **13**, **14**, **15**, **16**, **17**, **22**
favelas **7**, 8
festivals **26**, **27**
flag **28**

floods **8**
food **14–17**
 brigadeiros **16–17**
 coconuts **15**
 coffee 8, 23
 fruit 14, 15, 21, 23
 sugar 8, **23**
 vegetables 14, 15, 21
free time **24–25**

games **13**

high-rise buildings **6**, **7**, **10**
holidays 20, 26
homes **4**, **6**, **7**, **10–13**

lagoon **7**, **10**, 12
languages 4, 19, 28

mountains **5**, 28
music 27, **29**

plantations 8, 23
population 28

rain forest **5**, 8
religions **26–27**, 29
rivers **5**, **29**

school **7**, **18–21**
shops **7**, **15**, 23
sports
 football **9**
 surfing 24
 volleyball **24**

tourism 22, 23
transportation 7, **18**
tropics **5**, 8

university **7**, **22**

weather **8–9**
wildlife **25**, **29**
work **22–23**